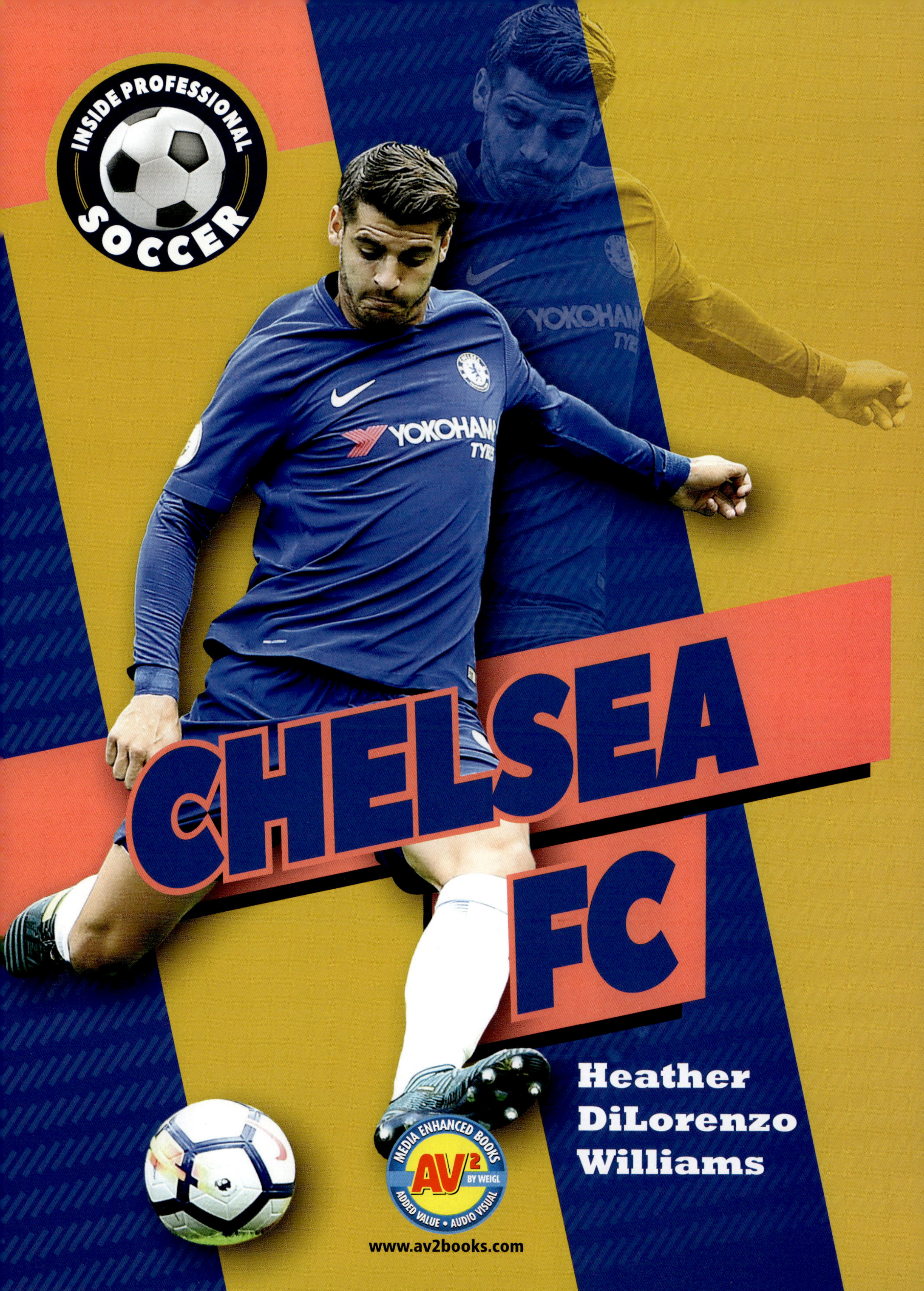
INSIDE PROFESSIONAL
SOCCER
CHELSEA
FC
Heather
DiLorenzo
Williams
MEDIA ENHANCED BOOKS
AV2 BY WEIGL
ADDED VALUE • AUDIO VISUAL
www.av2books.com

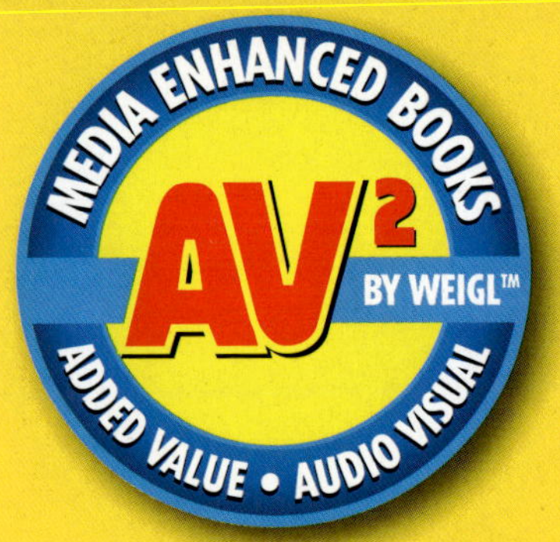

Go to www.av2books.com, and enter this book's unique code.

BOOK CODE

AVU44329

AV² by Weigl brings you media enhanced books that support active learning.

AV² provides enriched content that supplements and complements this book. Weigl's AV² books strive to create inspired learning and engage young minds in a total learning experience.

Your AV² Media Enhanced books come alive with...

Audio
Listen to sections of the book read aloud.

Key Words
Study vocabulary, and complete a matching word activity.

Video
Watch informative video clips.

Quizzes
Test your knowledge.

Embedded Weblinks
Gain additional information for research.

Slide Show
View images and captions, and prepare a presentation.

Try This!
Complete activities and hands-on experiments.

... and much, much more!

Published by AV² by Weigl
350 5th Avenue, 59th Floor
New York, NY 10118
Website: www.av2books.com

Library of Congress Control Number: 2018968480

ISBN 978-1-7911-0604-1 (hardcover)
ISBN 978-1-7911-0605-8 (multi-user eBook)
ISBN 978-1-7911-0606-5 (single-user eBook)

Printed in Guangzhou, China
1 2 3 4 5 6 7 8 9 0 23 22 21 20 19

022019
102318

Project Coordinator: John Willis   Designer: Terry Paulhus

Every reasonable effort has been made to trace ownership and to obtain permission to reprint copyright material. The publishers would be pleased to have any errors or omissions brought to their attention so that they may be corrected in subsequent printings.

The publisher acknowledges Alamy, Getty Images, iStock, and Wikimedia as its primary image suppliers for this title.

CONTENTS

Introduction

Soccer is called football in most European countries. Chelsea Football **Club** (FC) is one of London's most exciting soccer teams. Chelsea FC is part of Great Britain's Premier League. More people watch Premier League soccer games on television than any other sport.

Chelsea's stadium is located near Royal Hospital Chelsea, a hospital for **pensioners**. The hospital's residents were some of the team's first supporters. They gave the team its first nickname, the Pensioners. They still come to games in their long red military coats and cheer for Chelsea.

Chelsea's biggest rival is another London team called Arsenal FC. Both teams consider themselves to be the best in London. The two teams have played each other more than 170 times. They were the first two teams in professional soccer to wear numbers on their jerseys. Although the teams have a lot in common, there are many unique things that set Chelsea apart from Arsenal and London's other teams.

N'Golo Kanté has won the Premier League championship with two different teams, Chelsea and Leicester City.

Some of soccer's greatest players have worn the number 10. Chelsea star Eden Hazard has been compared to another renowned number 10, Lionel Messi.

CHELSEA FC

Arena Stamford Bridge

Division Premier League

Head Coach Maurizio Sarri

Location Chelsea, London, England

FIFA Club World Cups 0 (runners-up in 2012)

Nicknames the Blues, the Pensioners

6 Premier League Championships

8 Football Association (FA) Cup Wins

28 Total Trophies

1 Home Stadium

9 Players with 100-plus Goals

History

Chelsea was in deep debt when Ken Bates bought the team for £1 ($1.50). The purchase price was just a symbolic gesture that meant ownership of the team had been transferred to Bates.

In 1904, businessman Gus Mears bought a stadium in Fulham, England. There was already a soccer team called Fulham FC. So, in 1905, Mears founded a new soccer team to play in the stadium. He named his team Chelsea Football Club after the neighborhood next to Fulham. The Mears family owned Chelsea for almost 80 years.

Chelsea was the first London team to reach England's FA Cup Final in 1915. However, Chelsea did not win a **title** in its first 50 years. Fans did not seem to mind. Chelsea quickly became one of the most supported clubs in England. In 1955, Chelsea won the Premier League title for the first time. The team won its first FA Cup in 1970 and a major European title, the European Cup Winners' Cup, in 1971.

In 1982, businessman Ken Bates purchased Chelsea from the Mears family for £1, or about $1.50. Bates invested large amounts of money in the stadium and to hire players from other countries. In 2003, Bates sold Chelsea for £140 million ($180 million). Russian billionaire Roman Abramovich transformed Chelsea into a successful team. Abramovich renovated Chelsea's stadium. He also improved Chelsea's roster and coaching staff. In 2013, Chelsea became the only British team to win all three major European titles when they won the Union of European Football Associations' (UEFA's) Europa League.

Chelsea owner Roman Abramovich has invested more than $1 billion in the club since taking it over.

The Arena

A statue of Chelsea legend **Peter Osgood** stands outside the entrance of the stadium. Many fans **salute** the statue as they make their way inside.

The 1994 renovation of Stamford Bridge included removal of the stadium's running track. It transformed the stadium into a dedicated soccer arena.

Stamford Bridge opened in 1877, almost 30 years before Gus Mears founded Chelsea FC. Originally, it was mostly used for track and field events. It also hosted dog races and the world championship of a Scottish game called **shinty**. When Mears purchased the stadium, he installed a long stand with seating for several thousand people on one side of the field. The other three sides were **terraces** for standing.

Stamford Bridge was renovated in 1994. The renovation provided fans with covered seating on all four sides. Each of the four seating sections has a unique name and seating capacity. The Matthew Harding Stand is named after a former Chelsea director. The Shed End, East Stand, and West Stand make up the remaining sections.

Stamford Bridge seats almost 42,000 people. It includes an adjacent hotel, apartments, a museum, and a live music venue called Under the Bridge. In recent years, Chelsea explored building a larger stadium. The team also considered a major renovation of Stamford Bridge. But neither option has moved forward, and Stamford Bridge remains the home of the Blues.

The Chelsea FC Museum is the largest soccer museum in London.

Where They Play

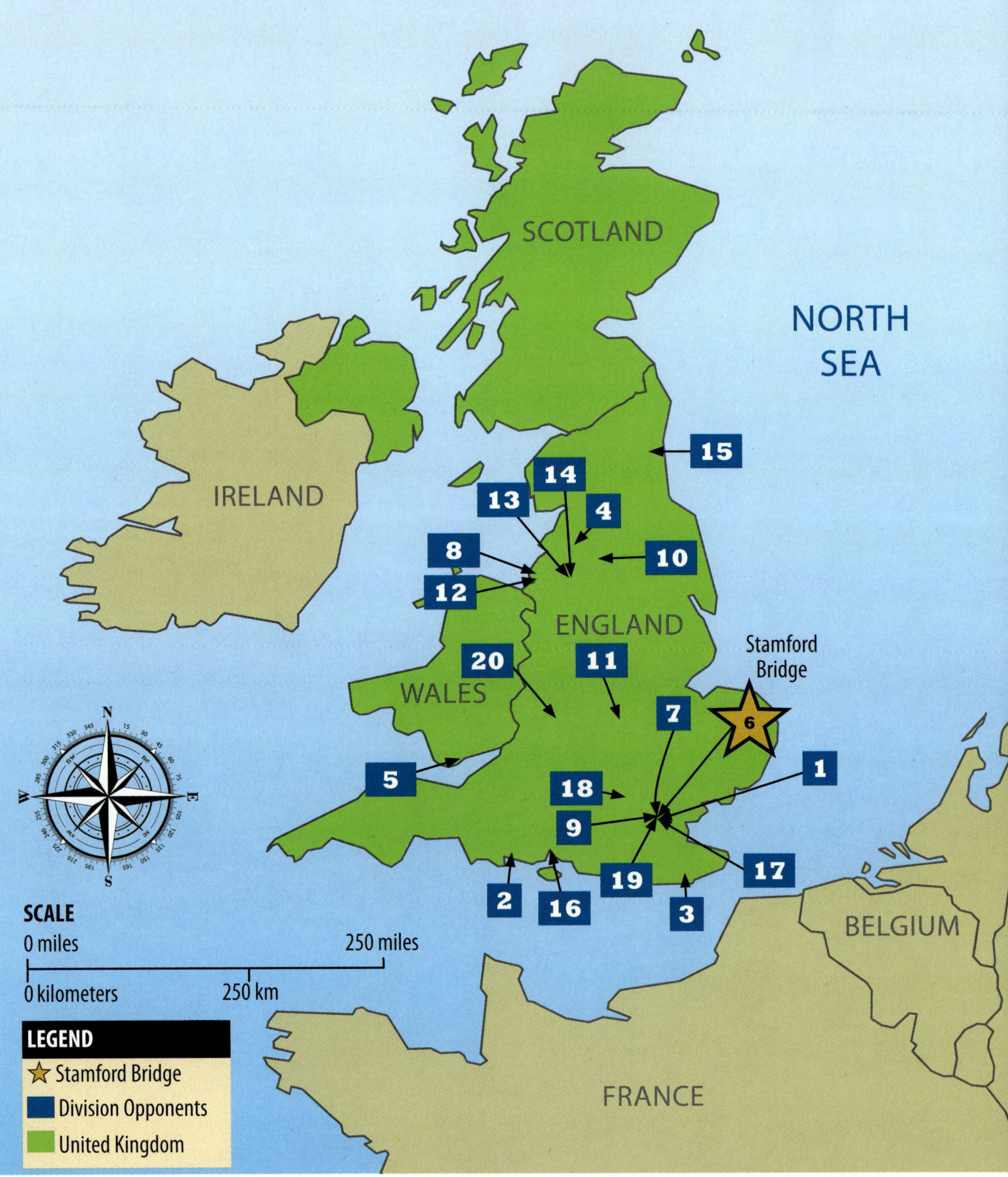

SWEDEN

FINLAND

NORWAY

DENMARK

GERMANY

Arena
Stamford Bridge

Location
London, England

Broke Ground
1876

Completed
April 28, 1877

Field Design
The pitch is surrounded by four covered seating areas made up of mostly royal blue seats, with some white seats spelling out the word "CHELSEA."

Features

- Original stadium terraces were formed from Piccadilly subway line's excavated dirt.
- Ken Bates once suggested an electric fence be built around the pitch to keep fans off the field.
- The wall of Shed End is the only remaining part of the original 1877 stadium.

2018 PREMIER LEAGUE TEAMS

1 Arsenal *(Highbury, London, England)*
2 Bournemouth *(Bournemouth, England)*
3 Brighton and Hove Albion *(Brighton and Hove, England)*
4 Burnley *(Burnley, England)*
5 Cardiff City *(Cardiff, Wales)*
★ 6 Chelsea *(West London, England)*
7 Crystal Palace *(South London, England)*
8 Everton *(Liverpool, England)*
9 Fulham *(Hammersmith and Fulham, England)*
10 Huddersfield Town *(Huddersfield, England)*
11 Leicester City *(Leicester, England)*
12 Liverpool *(Liverpool, England)*
13 Manchester City *(Manchester, England)*
14 Manchester United *(Manchester, England)*
15 Newcastle United *(Newcastle-upon-Tyne, England)*
16 Southampton *(Southampton, England)*
17 Tottenham Hotspur *(North London, England)*
18 Watford *(Watford, England)*
19 West Ham United *(East London, England)*
20 Wolverhampton Wanderers *(Wolverhampton, England)*

The Uniforms

Chelsea has worn a white jersey with blue accents for away matches in the past. Yokohama Rubber Company has sponsored the Blues' jerseys since 2015.

Chelsea's first uniforms consisted of pale blue jerseys, white shorts, and dark black or blue socks. Royal blue later replaced pale blue and became the team's main color. Today Chelsea's typical home **kit** is royal blue jerseys and shorts with white socks.

Chelsea's away uniform is gold with royal blue socks. A third kit is light blue and orange. There have been other unique uniforms and color combinations in the team's past. Red has been featured as an accent, a sock color, and sometimes the entire uniform. One gray and orange kit is considered one of the most unsightly uniforms in soccer history.

Five different crests have decorated Chelsea's game-day programs and jerseys. The crest has featured a bearded pensioner, a lion, and simple club initials. Today's crest has a lion holding a staff in the center. The crest is mostly royal blue with red roses and soccer balls, accented with gold and white.

Despite being worn by soccer stars including Ruud Gullit and Michael Duberry, Chelsea's 1994 to 1996 away kit is rated one of the sport's worst of all time.

Goalie Gear

Kepa's transfer fee to leave Athletic Club Bilbao and sign with Chelsea was more than $90 million, making him the most expensive goalkeeper in the world. He paid the fee himself in order to become Chelsea's goalie.

Goalkeepers must stand out from field players and officials. Goalies usually wear long sleeves. Their jerseys are a different color from their team's uniforms. Goalies can wear shorts or pants if they choose. Goalkeeper jerseys and pants sometimes have protective pads built into them.

Most goalkeepers wear special goalkeeping gloves. These gloves have rubbery surfaces to help the goalkeeper grip the ball. Some goalkeeper gloves contain plastic spines to protect the goalie's hands from injuries. There are also some goalkeepers who wear special helmets.

Chelsea's goalkeeper is Kepa Arrizabalaga, known simply as Kepa. He joined the team at the start of the 2018 season. Kepa is only 24, but he plays like a seasoned goalkeeper. He is known for keeping his cool under pressure. In his first game ever, Kepa stopped a shot by Cristiano Ronaldo that was 12 yards (11 meters) from the goal. Kepa wears a lime green jersey for Chelsea.

Willy Caballero, Chelsea's second goalie, once made three saves in a penalty kick shootout during the League Cup Final while playing for Manchester City. This rare feat gave Caballero a reputation as one of the Premier League's best goalkeepers.

The Coaches

Maurizio Sarri never played soccer professionally. He was a banker before he became a soccer coach.

Sarri's coaching style of fast-moving, quick passes is known as "Sarri-ball" or "liquid football" in the professional soccer world.

Chelsea has had 32 permanent coaches and several temporary coaches. Some led the team for decades and others only coached a few games. A few former Chelsea players have gone on to coach the team. Chelsea's longest-serving coach was David Calderhead. He coached the team for 26 years. The current head coach of Chelsea is Maurizio Sarri. He was appointed at the start of the 2018 season.

MAURIZIO SARRI Maurizio Sarri started coaching soccer in Italy in 1990. Chelsea is his first team outside of Italy. In his short time with Chelsea, Sarri has implemented the biggest change in style of play the team has ever seen. Sarri likes to play his team close together on the field to avoid big gaps in offense and defense. This allows them to maintain possession of the ball during the game.

JOSÉ MOURINHO José Mourinho is considered one of the greatest soccer coaches in the world. He is known for his unique coaching methods and tactics. Mourinho has a reputation for making quick changes in a game based on how his players are playing. When he was hired at Chelsea in 2004, Mourinho referred to himself in an interview as "a top manager." He went on to prove himself right. Mourinho is the club's most successful coach of all time.

TOMMY DOCHERTY Tommy "the Doc" Docherty had just retired from playing when he became Chelsea's head coach in 1962. He was known to be unpredictable and had a big temper. However, Docherty brought innovative tactics and training to the team. Chelsea found success under his leadership.

Fans Around the World

Chelsea fans know hundreds of songs and chants that celebrate their team, such as "Blue is the Colour," "Ten Men Went to Mow," "Over Land and Sea," and "Blue Flag."

Chelsea FC is one of the most supported soccer teams in the world. There are official Chelsea supporter clubs in several countries. They include the Sydney Supporters' Club in Australia, the Saudi Arabia Supporters' Club, and the New York Blues Supporters' Club in the United States. Actor Will Ferrell and chef Gordon Ramsay are both fans of the Blues.

Chelsea's Twitter account has more than 12 million followers. More than 47 million people keep up with the team on Facebook. Fans can watch game highlights and behind-the-scenes videos on the team's YouTube channel. An official Chelsea FC app lets fans keep up with games in real time.

On game days, Chelsea fans parade down Fulham Road into Stamford Bridge. Fans sing songs and chants. They wear special Chelsea scarves and hold up huge banners and signs during matches.

Fan Traditions

#1 Thanks to a song called "Celery" that was written by a Chelsea supporter, fans once threw stalks of celery at the opposing team during matches. Today, fans only throw celery during Chelsea victory parades.

#2 Many fans walk the Chelsea FC trail at nearby Brompton Cemetery right after matches to pay tribute to famous Chelsea-related graves.

Legends of the Past

Many great players have suited up for Chelsea FC. A few of them have become icons of the team and the city it represents.

Position: Goalkeeper
Years in Pro Soccer: 1999–Present (2004–2015 with Chelsea)
Born: May 20, 1982
Plzeň, Czechoslovakia

Petr Čech

Petr Čech began his record-breaking 11-year career at Chelsea in 2004. He has the best record of any goalkeeper who has played for Chelsea. During his first season with Chelsea, the Blues won their first title in 50 years. Čech went on to win 12 more titles with the team. In 2006, Čech experienced a life-threatening head injury after colliding with an opposing player. He now wears a trademark protective helmet that was specially designed for him. Čech also played goalkeeper in 124 matches for the Czech Republic national team. He left Chelsea in 2015 to play for rival Arsenal.

Gianfranco Zola

Forward Gianfranco Zola was mentored by the legendary Diego Maradona before signing with Chelsea. He had already won four trophies in Italy before he helped Chelsea win its first major title in 26 years. Chelsea went on to win three more major trophies with Zola's help. Known for his creative goal-scoring, Zola scored 80 goals in 312 games at Chelsea. Zola was the team's player of the year twice and was voted the club's greatest player ever. He now serves as the team's assistant coach.

Position: Forward
Years in Pro Soccer: 1984–2005 (1996–2003 with Chelsea)
Born: July 5, 1966, Oliena, Italy

Didier Drogba

Didier Drogba is considered one of soccer's greatest forwards. He is known for his powerful shots, speed, and accuracy. Drogba's speed and 6-foot, 2-inch (188-centimeter) height make him difficult to defend against. He scored a total of 164 goals in 381 total appearances for Chelsea, making him the club's fourth all-time highest scorer. Drogba led Chelsea to 14 trophies, including the club's first-ever UEFA Champions League title, where he scored the winning goal. He scored 10 goals in 10 different major finals for Chelsea. Drogba is the second-leading African scorer of all time, and has been named African player of the year twice.

Position: Forward
Years in Pro Soccer: 1998–Present (2004–2012 and 2014–2015 with Chelsea)
Born: March 11, 1978, Abidjan, Ivory Coast

Peter Osgood

Nicknamed the "King of Stamford Bridge," Peter Osgood played in his first game for Chelsea at age 17. Osgood was known as a versatile, creative player. He could score goals in a variety of ways and from many locations on the field. Osgood helped Chelsea become competitive on the European stage for the first time in the club's history. Osgood scored in every round of the 1970 FA Cup and helped Chelsea win the final for the first time. Stamford Bridge's statue of Osgood was erected in 2010 to honor his contributions to Chelsea.

Position: Forward
Years in Pro Soccer: 1964–1979 (1964–1974 and 1978–1979 with Chelsea)
Born: February 20, 1947 Windsor, England

Stars of Today

Today's Chelsea FC team is made up of many young, talented players who have proven that they are among the best in the league.

Eden Hazard

Eden Hazard is considered one of the best players in the world. Playing as both a **midfielder** and a forward, Hazard is known for speed, ball control, and for running past **defenders**. He has led Chelsea to two Premier League titles, the FA Cup, and the UEFA Europa League title. His entire family, including both parents, played pro or semi-pro soccer. Hazard has played 310 games and scored 97 goals for Chelsea. He is the captain of the Belgian national team and led Belgium to the semi-final of the 2018 World Cup. Hazard is also a co-owner of the newly formed North American Soccer League team San Diego 1904 FC.

Position: Midfielder/Forward
Years in Pro Soccer: 2007–Present (Joined Chelsea in 2012)
Born: January 7, 1991, La Louvière, Belgium

N'Golo Kanté

N'Golo Kanté played at Premier League rival Leicester City before signing with Chelsea. Kanté is known for clean tackles, intercepting the ball, and near-perfect passes. He averages an almost 90 percent pass accuracy. Kanté is skilled at defending and switching immediately to offense when he gains possession. A French teammate praised his ability to run for 90 straight minutes, claiming he "can run for 11 players." Kanté is a member of the French national team. He played all 90 minutes of all seven 2018 World Cup games, including the final in which France defeated Croatia 4-2.

Position: Midfielder
Years in Pro Soccer: 2012–Present (Joined Chelsea in 2016)
Born: March 29, 1991, Paris, France

Willian Borges da Silva

Willian Borges da Silva, known simply as Willian, played in Russia, Ukraine, and his home country of Brazil before landing at Chelsea. Club supporters were so eager for him to sign with Chelsea that they wrote a song about him before he ever stepped onto the pitch. Willian is known for explosive speed and footwork, including fakes and tricks typical of the Brazilian style of play. He often uses a trick called "elastico," in which a player changes the ball's direction with the same foot in a quick motion. Willian has played 248 games and scored 46 goals for Chelsea. He also plays on the Brazilian national team and played in the 2018 World Cup.

Position: Midfielder/Forward
Years in Pro Soccer: 2006–Present (Joined Chelsea in 2013)
Born: August 9, 1988, Ribeirão Pires, São Paulo, Brazil

César Azpilicueta

César Azpilicueta is a skilled defender who is comfortable playing the right, left, or center of the field. Azpilicueta's teammates nicknamed him "Dave" due to his lengthy last name. The nickname originated from a British television show in which one character cannot remember another's name and calls him Dave instead. Azpilicueta averages a 75 percent tackle success rate. He is known for winning and possessing the ball. Azpilicueta has played 291 games and scored eight goals for Chelsea. He helped the Blues win five trophies, including the 2013 Europa League. Azpilicueta has been a part of Spain's national team since 2013.

Position: Defender
Years in Pro Soccer: 2006–Present (Joined Chelsea in 2012)
Born: August 28, 1989, Pamplona, Spain

All-Time Records

211
Most All-Time Goals Scored

Frank Lampard holds the record for most all-time goals scored for Chelsea, with 211.

13
Most Goals in a Home Match

Chelsea scored a record 13 goals in a home match against Jeunesse Hautcharage in 1971.

795
Most Games Played

Ron Harris played a record 795 games for Chelsea.

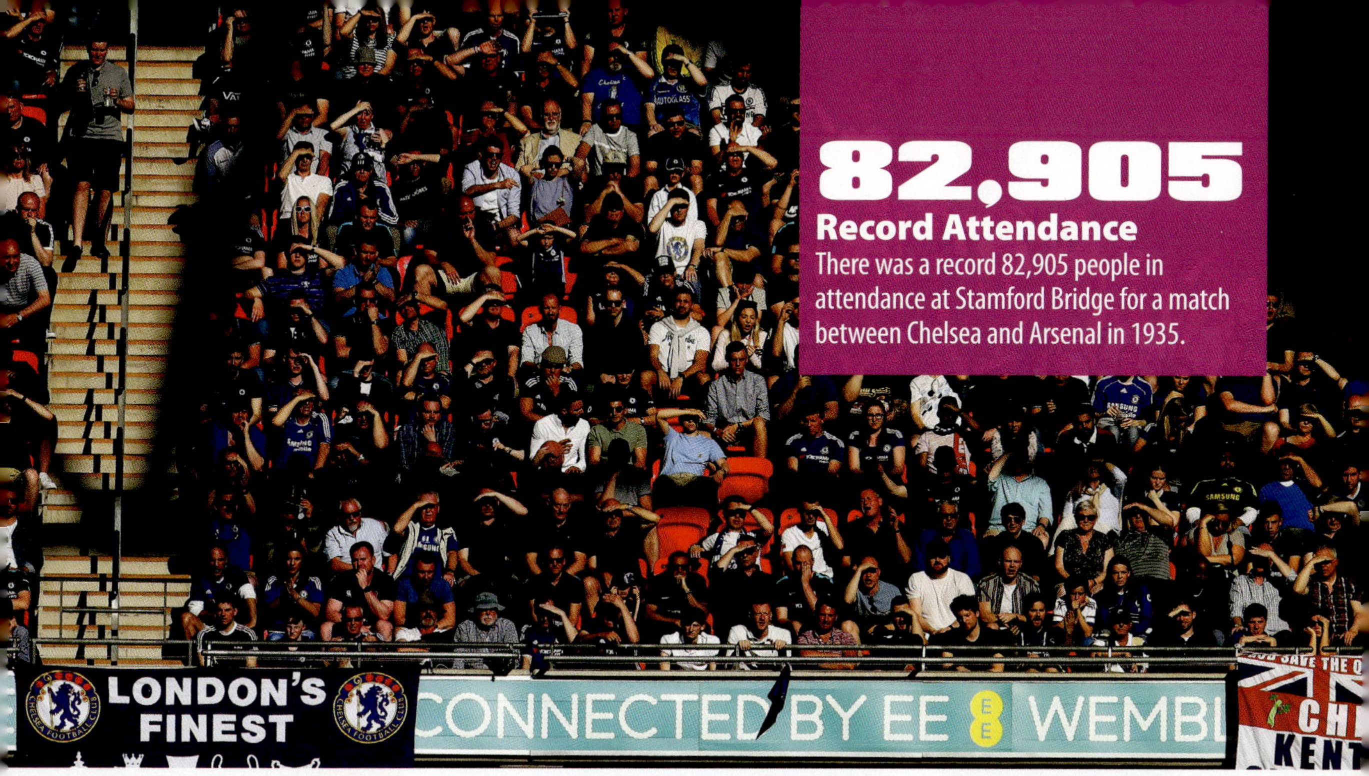

82,905

Record Attendance

There was a record 82,905 people in attendance at Stamford Bridge for a match between Chelsea and Arsenal in 1935.

86

Longest Win Streak at Home

From 2004 to 2008, Chelsea played 86 unbeaten home matches, an English club soccer record.

Timeline

Throughout the team's history, Chelsea FC has had many memorable events that have become defining moments for the team and its fans.

1876
Stamford Bridge is constructed in Fulham, London, England.

1955
After making changes to modernize Chelsea, Coach Ted Drake leads the team to its first league championship.

1870 | 1900 | 1910 | 1920 | 1930 | 1940 | 1950

In 1904, Gus Mears buys Stamford Bridge with plans to make it a soccer venue.

1928
Chelsea and Arsenal become the first club teams to wear numbered jerseys in a game.

1935
The team records its highest home attendance in history. The record remains the fourth largest turnout for a Premier League match.

1982
Businessman Ken Bates buys a struggling Chelsea club for £1 ($1.50).

2003
Ken Bates sells Chelsea to Russian businessman Roman Abramovich for £140 million ($180 million).

The Future
With a new coach on the field, Chelsea's future is bright. Changes in style of play and building on the strength of the team's roster could mean big wins for the current and future seasons. As one of the Premier League's most popular teams, Chelsea continues to draw devoted fans to Stamford Bridge, and to fan sites and social media around the globe.

1960 | 1970 | 1980 | 1990 | 2000 | 2010 | 2020

In 1971, Chelsea wins its first European title, the UEFA Cup Winners' Cup.

2018
Chelsea wins its sixth Premier League title.

Write a Biography

Life Story

A person's life story can be the subject of a book. This kind of book is called a biography. Biographies often describe the lives of people who have achieved great success. These people may be alive today, or they may have lived many years ago. Reading a biography can help you learn more about a great person.

Get the Facts

Use research in the library and on the internet to find out more about your favorite soccer player. Learn as much about him or her as you can. What position does he or she play? What are his or her statistics in important categories? Has he or she set any records? Also, be sure to write down key events in the person's life. What was his or her childhood like? What has he or she accomplished off the field? Is there anything else that makes this person special or unusual?

Use the Concept Web

A concept web is a useful research tool. Read the questions in the concept web on the following page. Answer the questions in your notebook. Your answers will help you write a biography.

Concept Web

Adulthood
- Where does this individual currently reside?
- Does he or she have a family?

Your Opinion
- What did you learn from the books you read in your research?
- Would you suggest these books to others?
- Was anything missing from these books?

Childhood
- Where and when was this person born?
- Describe his or her parents, siblings, and friends.
- Did this person grow up in unusual circumstances?

Accomplishments off the Field
- What is this person's life's work?
- Has he or she received awards or recognition for accomplishments?
- How have this person's accomplishments served others?

Write a Biography

Help and Obstacles
- Did this individual have a positive attitude?
- Did he or she receive help from others?
- Did this person have a mentor?
- Did this person face any hardships?
- If so, how were the hardships overcome?

Accomplishments on the Field
- What records does this person hold?
- What key games and plays have defined his or her career?
- What are this person's stats in categories important to his or her position?

Work and Preparation
- What was this person's education?
- What was his or her work experience?
- How does this person work?
- What is the process he or she uses?

Trivia Time

Take this quiz to test your knowledge of Chelsea FC. The answers are printed upside down under each question.

1 Chelsea and what team were the first to wear numbered jerseys?

A. Arsenal FC

2 How many Chelsea players have scored more than 100 goals?

A. Nine

3 What honor did Chelsea achieve for the first time in 1955?

A. Winning the Premier League title

4 How much did Ken Bates pay to purchase Chelsea in 1982?

A. £1 ($1.50)

5 The world championship of what Scottish game was played at Stamford Bridge before Gus Mears converted it into a soccer stadium?

A. Shinty

6 What vegetable is associated with Chelsea FC fans?

A. Celery

7 What animal is featured on Chelsea's logo?

A. A lion

8 Who was Chelsea's longest-serving coach?

A. David Calderhead

9 What was coach Maurizio Sarri's job before he became a soccer coach?

A. Banker

Key Words

club: an athletic team or organization

defenders: also called "backs," players who play in front of the goal and stop the other team from scoring

forward: a player on a soccer team who normally plays closest to the opponent's goal and tries to score goals

goalkeepers: also called "goalies," the players responsible for keeping the ball from going into the goal and the only players who are allowed to pick up the ball

kit: the standard attire worn by soccer players, including a jersey, shorts, socks, and shin guards

midfielder: a soccer player who plays between the forwards and defenders and can take either a defensive or offensive role

pensioners: retired British soldiers

shinty: a Scottish game resembling field hockey, played by two teams of 12 with curved sticks and a leather-covered cork ball

terraces: areas in stadiums specifically designated for standing

title: championship

Index

Log on to www.av2books.com

AV² by Weigl brings you media enhanced books that support active learning. Go to www.av2books.com, and enter the special code found on page 2 of this book. You will gain access to enriched and enhanced content that supplements and complements this book. Content includes video, audio, weblinks, quizzes, a slide show, and activities.

AV² Online Navigation

Audio
Listen to sections of the book read aloud.

Book Pages
AV² pages directly correspond to pages in the book.

Video
Watch informative video clips.

Embedded Weblinks
Gain additional information for research.

Key Words
Study vocabulary, and complete a matching word activity.

Try This!
Complete activities and hands-on experiments.

Quizzes
Test your knowledge.

Slide Show
View images and captions, and prepare a presentation.

AV² was built to bridge the gap between print and digital. We encourage you to tell us what you like and what you want to see in the future.

Sign up to be an AV² Ambassador at www.av2books.com/ambassador.

Due to the dynamic nature of the Internet, some of the URLs and activities provided as part of AV² by Weigl may have changed or ceased to exist. AV² by Weigl accepts no responsibility for any such changes. All media enhanced books are regularly monitored to update addresses and sites in a timely manner. Contact AV² by Weigl at 1-866-649-3445 or av2books@weigl.com with any questions, comments, or feedback.